St. Thomas Aquinas
The Catholic Center at Purdue

The Way of the Cross
Stations of the Cross

Paintings by: *Katie Schmid*
Reflections by: *Dominican Friars of the Province of St. Albert the Great*

NEW PRIORY PRESS
EXPLORING THE DOMINICAN VISION

Paintings copyright © 2011 Katie Schmid. Used with permission.
www.katieschmid.com
Photographs by Brent Russell

Copyright © 2014 Dominican Province of St. Albert the Great (U.S.A.).
All rights reserved. Published by New Priory Press,
1910 South Ashland Avenue, Chicago, IL 60608   www.NewPrioryPress.com

For more information about St. Thomas Aquinas, the Catholic Center at Purdue, visit www.boilercatholics.org.

For more information about the Dominican Order and the Dominican Friars of the Province of St. Albert the Great, visit www.opcentral.org.

Contents

Preface		*iv*
How to Pray the Stations		*v*
Introduction		2
I.	Christ is Condemned to Death	4
II.	Christ Embraces His Cross	6
III.	Christ Falls the First Time	8
IV.	Christ Meets His Sorrowful Mother	10
V.	Simon Helps Christ Carry His Cross	12
VI.	Veronica Wipes the Face of Christ	14
VII.	Christ Falls the Second Time	16
VIII.	Christ Meets the Women of Jerusalem	18
IX.	Christ Falls the Third Time	20
X.	Christ is Stripped of His Garments	22
XI.	Christ is Nailed to the Cross	24
XII.	The Crucifixion	26
XIII.	Christ is Taken Down from the Cross and Placed in His Mother's Arms	28
XIV.	Christ is Laid in the Tomb	30
Concluding Prayer		32

PREFACE

From the earliest days of the Church, Christians have repeated the account of Jesus' passion, death, and resurrection. Many desired to see first-hand the sites in Jerusalem where Jesus spent the last hours before his crucifixion. Such a pilgrimage on "the Way of the Cross" (in Latin, the *Via Crucis*) made the familiar stories more tangible and personal. As Christianity spread further throughout the world, many were unable to visit the holy sites, yet the desire to somehow replicate this devotional experience continued. This gave rise to what are commonly known as the Stations of the Cross, a series of 14 images representing key moments in Christ's Passion. Promoted especially by the Francisans, since the medieval period it has become common in Catholic churches throughout the world to include a series of these stations on the walls of the church. As a popular devotion, communal meditation on the Way of the Cross is most common during the season of Lent, especially on Fridays, the day of the Lord's passion and death.

The images of the Way of the Cross featured here are the original work of painter Katie Schmid. The series of paintings is on permanent display at the St. Thomas Aquinas Catholic Center at Purdue University, in West Lafayette, Indiana.

Inspired by these moving images of Jesus' passion and death, the Dominican Friars of the Province of St. Albert the Great, U.S.A., have collaborated in composing a brief reflection and prayer for each station. This book may be used for private devotion or with a group.

Many thanks to all who contributed to the making of this reflection book. We hope that this prayer resource may draw many closer to Christ as we walk with him on the Way of the Cross.

How to Pray the Stations

Since the goal and purpose of prayer is deepening our union with God, it is well to remember that the pictures and words found here are simply a means to this end. Thus, when anything in the image or reflection moves us either to converse with the Lord, ponder a mystery or simply rest in God's presence, we should follow this inspiration of the Holy Spirit without feeling bound to keep reading the reflection. The reflection's job is to move us to prayer, and when we are done following a particular inspiration we can then return to finish the reflection.

There are two types of benefits to be sought in each station. Every part of Christ's life aims to give us some instruction and to bestow some grace for the healing and strengthening of our hearts. Instruction is for the guidance of the mind, and grace is to buoy up our hearts for the carrying out of God's will. For example, we can learn from one of Jesus' falls always to rise up after we've fallen, but just as importantly, in getting back up Jesus merited for us the strength we need to follow suit. It is one thing to know what should be done; it is another to have the fortitude or patience actually to do it. Christ offers us both types of help in every mystery of His life.

The fundamental grace to be desired is conversion of heart. The more we turn away from sin and toward the Lord, the healthier our souls become. "By his wounds we are healed" (Is 53:5). The wounds in the Lord's Sacred Head from the crown of thorns may atone for our sins of thought and heal the disorder they've bred in our minds. When interiorly wounded by hatred, Jesus' act of forgiveness on the Cross may alleviate the vengeful bitterness in our hearts. And so forth… Whatever infirmity our souls may experience, we can find in Christ's Passion a perfect and abundant remedy. The more we study it, the more treasures we will discover. Let us show the Lord our gratitude by often making use of so priceless a gift.

Dedicated to M. L.
in gratitude for her inspiration

The Way of the Cross

*We adore you, O Christ
and we bless you.*

*Because by your Holy Cross
you have redeemed the world.*

INTRODUCTION

The Son of God came to earth to do one thing, ultimately, and that is to reveal to us who God is. Because God is Love itself, and love is revealed most effectively by actions, God's self-revelation involved saving us from eternal perdition and winning for us the gift of eternal life. God had already testified "in partial and various ways to our ancestors through the prophets" that He loves us, and He had shown this love for humanity by accomplishing great and wondrous deeds such as freeing the Israelites from Egypt. (Heb 1:1) But since this was not sufficient to convey the depths of God's love, He came to us in person to give yet more dramatic evidence of His overwhelming compassion. Thus, when faced with physical suffering, Christ healed; when faced with ignorance and confusion, He taught; and when faced with possession, He expelled demons. Christ "went about doing good and healing all who were under the power of the devil." (Acts 10:38)

All this was but a prelude to Jesus' most heroic deed. "Greater love has no one than this, to lay down one's life for one's friends." (John 15:13) This was to be the culminating act—the most incontrovertible evidence of God's profound love for us. As we have seen, God had been helping us all along to get to know Who He is, so that we may enter into a deeper relationship with Him. One can hardly be in relationship with someone simply by knowing *about* the other person. Rather, it is necessary actually to have knowledge *of* the other by way of personal interaction. It is for this reason that Christ instituted the Holy Sacrifice of the Mass—which is the very sacrifice of Calvary, transcending time and space, made present in an unbloody manner on the altar—so that we could be present to and enter into the astounding drama of God's self-revelation in Christ's loving sacrifice on the Cross.

The devotion known as the Stations of the Cross is a means of studying in greater detail, with gratitude and wonder, the amazing demonstration of love Christ gave to us by laying down His life on our behalf. In order to derive from this devotion as much grace as

God wishes to give us, one further consideration will be helpful: Christ did not die just for humanity generically, as a corporate sum of people. In the words of St. Paul, Christ "loved *me* and gave himself for *me*." (Gal 2:20) This is all the more amazing when we remember that when Jesus was crucified, He had never met Saul of Tarsus. Yet the Apostle to the Gentiles is certain that Christ's sacrifice was made personally on his behalf. The Church recognizes in this a testimony to Christ's omniscience as the Second Person of the Trinity. God has knowledge of every detail of reality throughout all of history, and being eternal, Jesus had access even to knowledge of the future. Hence, when He freely laid down His life for us, Jesus knew by name and in detail each individual who would benefit from the crucifixion.

Nor was it the sheer multitude of the redeemed that moved Christ to make such a sacrifice, as though a smaller number of straying sheep would have been a less compelling reason to submit to being tortured & killed. The Lord loves each of us so completely that, had you or I been the only person on the face of the earth, Jesus would readily have endured all of His passion just for you or me. Indeed, He loves each of us as though we were the only one, and it is in this way that the Sacrifice of Calvary was made entirely for you, entirely for me.

Bearing these truths steadily in mind, and allowing them to sink into our hearts, we are enabled to appreciate something of the wonder and the mystery of what Christ has done for us. Mine and yours are the sins for which Jesus suffered, and ours is the redemption won at so great a price.

— *Timothy Combs, O.P.*

I — Christ is Condemned to Death

Jesus had said previously, on the occasion of his first miracle at Cana in Galilee, "My hour has not yet come" (Jn 2:4). Now the hour has come (Jn 12:23). Jesus had also said, "I did not come to condemn the world but to save the world" (Jn 12:47). Now the one who did not come to condemn the world is about to be condemned by the world. What irony! The one who instructed us not to judge is being judged.

But who are we to judge the Son of Man? It is true. We had made a choice in the Garden of Eden. Now a choice is given to us once again. Jesus or Barabbas? And the crowd will cry out: Crucify him. Pilate on behalf of us all passes the sentence – the sentence by which we are all sentenced. We have a need it seems to place blame, to flee our own responsibility, or to find a scapegoat. Are the Jewish people the guilty ones? Or was it Pilate and the Romans state? Was it not Judas who was most at fault? Or Peter himself who did not come to Christ's defense? No, rather, it is all of us who condemn Jesus to death when we too remain silent in the face of evil. Jesus who came to give us life (Jn 10:10) is condemned to death and judged by those who have no authority to judge. For us too, the hour has now come. The offer of repentance is here. We are given once again a choice. Let us let go of sin and let us open ourselves to the mercy of God.

— *Donald Goergen, O.P.*

Merciful and just Lord,
    free us from our slavery to sin
    and from our bondage to the things of this world.
We are sorry for having offended you.
Continue to pour forth upon us
    the grace of conversion
    and the gift of your Spirit,
so that we too may love one another
as you have loved us.
Amen.

II – Christ Embraces His Cross

In his ministry Jesus often spoke of this moment. He spoke of the time when He would take upon Himself and carry the burden of all our sin. He spoke of a debt to God the Father and price that only he could pay.

Taking the Cross, Jesus knew what part of His Cross actually belonged to each and every one of us as individuals. No part of that burden belonged to Him. Out of care and concern for each us, He accepted and embraced that Cross and love, which it truly represents. In this moment, none of us can hide from our responsibility. None of us can hide from the truth of those times when we have failed to live up to that to which we are called and meant to be in light of the Gospel. As sobering as this realization truly is, there is another side of this reality which far too often we overlook or even try to discount.

And this is simply that in taking up His Cross, Jesus is also saying to each and every one of us, without exception, that I love you and care for you enough that I am willing take this upon Myself so we can spend eternity together. None of us can escape this truth either. None of us can hide from God's love. Always remember that this is a moment that reverberates through all eternity. We are never alone in the burdens we must face. We are never carrying the weight of our mistakes on our shoulders alone, because Jesus has already accepted this task for us, and is still to this day willing to help us accept our crosses and carry them now.

— *Michail Ford, O.P.*

Lord Jesus,
    thank for accepting the burden
    of my debt to you.
Thank you for all of the love and forgiveness
    you showed us in the act of taking up your Cross.
Grant me the grace, the strength, and the courage
    to accept my burdens and responsibilities
    to you and your people
    and carry them knowing that you are with me
    in this and all that I do.
Amen.

III – Christ Falls the First Time

Jesus falls. I once heard the story of a young man who was praying in a chapel in the midst of a very difficult time in his life. Frustrated that he felt his prayer was going nowhere, he got up and said to God, "This is pointless—you're an all-powerful God off in heaven, what do you even know about my suffering?" As he turned to leave, he suddenly found himself face to face with an image of Jesus' Passion, and then he understood—God was not far from his suffering; He knew exactly what his pain meant.

Jesus falls. The Way of the Cross is not a show where an all-powerful Jesus pretends to suffer. His suffering is real. The cross makes him weak.

Jesus falls. For our sake, God not only became one of us, He became *weak*. Our sins—our rejections of God's offering of love—weighed heavy on Jesus' heart, and on His shoulders that bore the wood of the cross. Yet this is good news: God is not far when we fall. Perhaps we think that God is only there when we do the right thing, when our lives are going well; not so. Jesus enters into all the messiness of our humanity, all of our failures and sinfulness, and he embraces us right then and there, in the darkness, out of which he promises to guide us.

When we fall—which we shall—we need not hide from God, like Adam and Eve did in the Garden. Rather, we need only look to our side to see Jesus fallen beside us, and ask for His help to get back up again, knowing full-well that if (and likely when) we fall a second and third time, He will be there then as well.

— *Vincent Davila, O.P.*

Lord Jesus, all-powerful God;
    and also weak human being like me:
thank you for entering into all the messiness of my life,
    and loving me right in the midst of it.
Lord, when I fall, help me not to run from you
    in my shame, but let me find you there,
    sitting with me in the darkness when all else is gone.
Help me get up and continue carrying my cross
    right by your side,
    knowing that you will pick me up as many times
    as I fall.
In Your name, Amen.

IV – Christ Meets His Sorrowful Mother

As Jesus walks the way of the cross, he encounters Mary, his mother and our mother. She has not chosen to abandon Him as did His disciples but comes in love to be with her own son and suffering savior. Mary's love draws her to Jesus, even in His pain and suffering. She cannot abandon Him any more than He can be faithless towards us. For Jesus, it must have brought Him some consolation to know that at least her love had not failed. And yet this meeting too is part of Jesus' passion. Mary, full of grace, has opened her heart completely to love. In loving Jesus during His sorrowful passion, her heart is pierced by a sword, fulfilling the prophecy of Simeon (Luke 2:34-35). Mary is vulnerable and wounded because of her immense love, not in spite of it. Love is not a shield but an invitation. Jesus' love for His mother adds to the pain of this most sorrowful day. He grieves at seeing a mother, His mother, weep over the bruised and broken body of her only son.

Love draws us to one another. In love we share our joys and sorrows and receive them from others in order to make them our own. Only those who love can be hurt, but they are also the only ones who can know true joy. At the heart of the great spiritual work of comforting the afflicted is mercy. One heart sees the pain in another and takes it as its own. Knowing Jesus' own mercy towards us gives us the strength and courage to allow ourselves to be wounded in loving others.

— *Nicholas Monco, O.P.*

Dear Jesus, in carrying the cross
    you bore the pain and sins of the whole world,
    including the sorrow of your own mother's heart.
Give us eyes to see the sorrow that others carry
    and hearts that are generous and open
    to sharing your love with them.
May we be untiring in forgiving others
    and constantly aware of your mercy towards us.
As we journey to our true home of heaven,
    may your blessed mother protect us on our way.
Amen.

V – Simon Helps Christ Carry His Cross

Through a soft, gentle play of light, a strong, robust image is illuminated in this fifth station of the cross where Simon helps Jesus carry his cross. They walk shoulder to shoulder with Simon's arm and hand, with tensed fingers, purposely reaching around to rest on Jesus' upper back. The gesture does not seem intended to hold him up physically so much as to reassure Jesus emotionally that Simon's effort is not merely to be useful, but to be loving. Simon gives not merely the strength of his body to Jesus, but that of his heart.

Called from the anonymity of the crowd, how did Simon first feel? Startled? Afraid? Unworthy? Exposed? It was so much safer to be a spectator at this horrific journey of agony up Calvary's road. But now he is asked to get involved, to become publicly engaged in this man of mystery who has publicly preached to the mysteries of Simon's heart and multitudes of others.

Simon was chosen to participate in God's very life, in a particular way, as part of the powerful and poignant pageantry of God's love affair with humanity. What about me? Can I step out from the crowd to play the part that is mine in the divine love affair? Can I accept being chosen? But I'm unworthy. And what will people think? I'm afraid. I don't know if I can do what God is asking of me. What if I disappoint Jesus? What if I can't handle the weight of my part of the cross?

But then I remember that I don't have to carry it alone. Jesus asks me to carry it with him, alongside him, shoulder to shoulder. Each day the Crucified Christ of a million disguises comes before us in the emotionally-burdened, the physically–crippled, the psychologically-damaged, the guilt-laden, the spiritually-lost, the mentally-abandoned. Do we let them pass by, content to stay on the sidelines, or do we step out of the crowd and say: "Here I am Lord, send me?"

— Andrew-Carl Wisdom, O.P.

Lord, in Simon I see the unfolding of my own
    daily vocation, a call to love.
Let me not sit then as a spectator along the road of life,
    but hear the summons to step out and share the
    weight of another's cross.
When I shoulder the cross of another,
    I shoulder your cross.
When I walk with another in solidarity,
    I walk with you.
When I put my arm around another,
    I put my arm around you.
I become in this moment, with this person, in this life
circumstance, another YOU.

VI — Veronica Wipes the Face of Christ

Some people say this station isn't scriptural, but surely those first Christians who remembered the story were thinking of the words of the prophet Isaiah, "I gave my back to those who beat me, my cheeks to those who plucked my beard. I did not shield my face from buffets and spitting." (Is 50:6) It has the feel of a scripture story, and those Christians who first told it connected this woman with another whom we do know from the gospels. She had a hemorrhage and wanted only to touch the hem of the Lord's garment to be healed. So she was a woman who had been touched by Jesus and was trying to return the favor, or she was a stranger moved with compassion at another's suffering. In either case she was very, very brave.

Thoughtless of the crowd and the guards and all the rest she steps out. She offers her own veil, her head-covering, for the condemned man to wipe his face of blood and sweat and snot and spittle. She is ashamed at the way her friends and neighbors are treating another, and so she shames herself to offer him comfort. She reaches out to wipe his face; He reaches out and touches her heart.

And our hearts are touched also. He leaves an image on her handkerchief, but He leaves a deeper impression on her soul. He validates her kindness and her bravery with a priceless gift in order to show just how priceless was the gift she herself first offered. Her name is Veronica; that is, *vera icon*, or true image, not so much because of the sign which He left her, but because of the sign which she was to Him.

— *Dominic McManus, O.P.*

Stir up, O Lord, in our hearts and minds
    a constant devotion to your Holy Face.
Help us to see your glory reflected in our neighbors,
    especially those we are less inclined to see
    as we ought:
the poor and the weak, the drug-addled and addicted,
    the prostitute and the porn star,
    neglected and abused.
Help us to see them as you do, Lord,
    your own precious ones,
needing only what we all do: your own loving care.
Through Christ our Lord.
Amen.

VII — Christ Falls the Second Time

Jesus has just been unjustly mocked, derided, spit upon, and scourged. Why? Because of my sins. The innocent suffered for the guilty. He was already exhausted, not just physically, but mentally, emotionally, psychologically. So intense was his suffering that he began to sweat blood, and then was betrayed by a friend. But he suffered these indignities without complaint. He willingly accepted them for my sake. And now, he took on the extra burden of carrying his cross, knowing it would end in his crucifixion. Is it any wonder that he fell once again beneath the weight of the cross?

How would I have held up under these same circumstances? How do I hold up now when burdens come my way – the snub of a friend, the stub of a toe, a brief lapse in memory, an unjust accusation, or simply when things don't go my way? These are small inconveniences compared to what Jesus suffered for me. Yet, Jesus is merciful to me when I sin, when I seem to forget or ignore what he endured for me, when I, the guilty one, only think of my own convenience in life. Yet, still I complain.

— Joachim Culotta, O.P.

My Lord and my God, what you suffered for me should never be asked of anyone,
> especially one as innocent as you.

You willingly suffered these indignities for my sins.
Give me the strength of character to accept my burdens,
> to carry my crosses without complaining,
> to make lemonade when I am given lemons
> in this life.

At least, I know that my crosses will not end
> in crucifixion,

but in being united with you in heaven –
a small price to pay for such a glorious reward.
Amen.

VIII – Christ Meets the Women of Jerusalem

You feel the heavy weight of the cross, my sweet Jesus...the weight of my sins, and the sins of the world. You have been beaten, and tortured, and now you face the crowds of indifference and compassion mixed together in a sweltering mob of humanity...the sounds, the stench, the feel of the blood running down your back...and the ever increasing pain and exhaustion with every step. You can't seem to get your breath... always the dripping blood.

Who are these women? Do they really care for you? Are they mocking you?

You also meet me today...who am I? Do I really care for you? Am I mocking you?

Whatever the case, you meet them with compassion. Even in your ever increasing state of agony, you reach out to ease their suffering and you reach out to me today.

"Do not weep for me, weep for your children" you say to them...you say to me... "weep for yourselves."

Oh sweet Jesus, I know that you still suffer today in your mystical body. I know that so many children around the world are suffering in slavery, or trapped in war, or poverty, or orphans of AIDS. I know that so many women today are suffering from human trafficking, poverty, and discrimination. I know sweet Jesus, and yet I do little to help them. I know I could at the very least pray for them, but I often do not.

— *Simon-Felix Michalski, O.P.*

Jesus, give me your heart and teach me
   to really care about others in this world.
Give me sympathy, empathy, and compassion in action.
Soften my hard heart and harder head.
Give me the desire to begin to feel for the people
   who suffer so much from human-made disasters.
Help me to know that I am not innocent
   and that I have contributed to their suffering
   by my indifference,
   just as my sins have brought you to the cross.
Send Your Holy Spirit to us, O Lord,

IX — Christ Falls the Third Time

A few steps – then a stumble – he falls again. For the second time in life, Jesus is learning to walk. First as a child he learned to carry his weight, to crash to the ground, and to get back up over and over again. Then his mother could pick him up and kiss his bruises; now she watches helplessly. Indeed, this time everything is different. Jesus is carrying not just his own weight, but the weight of our transgressions. With each step, the heavy burden presses upon his back while he walks to Golgotha as our suffering Savior.

One thing, however, has not changed. Though he falls for a third time, Christ also gets back up for a third time. His pushes his way up from the ground with every ounce of power left in his body, limbs shaking in resistance. With each step he shows us the way to life; he refuses to stay on the ground under the cross of iniquity. He is struck down, but not destroyed. We too are challenged to get back up over and over again. To fall under sin, to mess up and wallow in our failure, is nothing but despair. This is the road to death instead of life. Conversely, the Way of the Cross is a story of hope – a promise of victory and the assurance that evil does not win. It is the story of Jesus' life ending just as it began. Once he learned to stand and walk to mother; now he learns to stand back up and run to the Father, carrying us every step of the way.

— *Joseph Trout, O.P.*

Source of strength and mercy,
    continually call us back to you
    whenever we fall down in sin.
Do not permit us to remain fallen,
    but send us your Spirit to stand again.
By your unending love, help us to turn away
    from all false promises of hope and fulfillment
    and continually follow after Jesus Christ.
Amen.

X — Christ is Stripped of His Garments

In taking away a person's clothes by force, one seeks to humiliate the other, not because the body is a shameful thing, but because to see a person's body is a matter of intimacy. Here, the enemies of Jesus want to disrobe him, not just to prepare him for execution, but as a way to say that underneath the garments of the traveling miracle worker is just a man of flesh and bones. Ironically, despite how horribly they have disfigured him, Jesus loses none of his dignity in this moment. In fact, his patience in suffering underscores the divine nature that his enemies cannot see.

Not long before this moment, James and John foolishly asked Jesus if they should call down destruction upon a town that had rejected the Gospel. They knew that God could do such a thing. Indeed, they felt he should, out of pride. But Jesus repeatedly illustrates—especially in the moment of his stripping—that God is not like us. So when the Word comes into the world, he comes not to conquer through violence, but through the transformative power of love. And so we see the Roman soldier, so full of movement and power with his muscles proudly bared. It seems as if he has the upper hand, that the light is on him. But we know that it is the man in the shadows so utterly alone, who is the image of true power. Not because he could have destroyed the soldier with a glance, but because he doesn't. Beautifully, it is out of love for that very soldier, and for that town James and John wanted to destroy, and for every human soul that would ever live, that the Son of God stands there stripped and still and silent.

— *Paul Byrd, O.P.*

Lord Jesus,
    we know that every human person,
    as a child of God, is endowed with great dignity;
help us then to more fully reflect that dignity
    by sending the Holy Spirit
    to teach us to be patient, when we are tried,
    to forgive, when we are wronged,
    and to love, when we are hated—
for it is only when we do as you would do
    that we truly fulfill our call to holiness.
We ask this in your holy name.
Amen.

XI – Christ is Nailed to the Cross

One thing that has impressed us so much about the life of Jesus upon this earth was his freedom. He entered the world into the Virgin's womb by his own initiative. He called disciples as he saw fit, always acting according to his own will. Speaking of his death, Jesus reminds us that it lies in his power alone to lay down his life and to raise it up again.

How very shocking, then, to see Jesus nailed to the Cross. Here we see what looks in every way to be the emblem of the loss of freedom. More than locking in prison or binding with ropes or chains, to be nailed is to have one's own body, one's very self, fixed in place. Where there was once the freedom to move as he willed, now there looks only to be the rigid sinews of the wood of the Cross, the unyielding iron of the nails. The soldiers seem to make of Christ's body a passive thing, the object of their action, capable itself of none.

Yet, this is where we have everything backwards. Jesus is not bound when he is nailed to the Cross, but rather supremely free. At this moment, when it seems that the Lord is prevented from doing anything of his own choosing, the truth is that what he chose in freedom out of love from before the dawn of time, he is now bringing about. By the mystery and paradox of the Passion, in being nailed in his hands and feet, Jesus is, by his sublime freedom, *blotting out the handwriting of ordinances that was against us, which was contrary to us, and* taking *it out of the way, nailing it to his Cross.* In suffering his vulnerable flesh to yield to the hard and inflexible iron of the nails, Jesus is actively shattering the hard and inflexible logic of our stony hearts, making them flesh once again, vulnerable to his love and mercy.

This is the freedom of the nails, the freedom of being fixed to the Cross of our Lord Jesus Christ, the freedom that comes from nailing our sins forever to that holy Tree, and joining our hearts to our gracious Savior in everlasting joy.

— *Dominic Holtz, O.P.*

By the holy iron of the Passion, O Lord,
    nail us to the saving wood of the Cross,
that being fixed there where the Lord Jesus Christ
    once died for the salvation of the world,
    and being made conformed to his sufferings,
we may rise with him on the Last Day
    and never be parted from him.
Through our Lord Jesus Christ, your Son,
    who lives and reigns with you and the Holy Spirit,
    one God, for ever and ever.
Amen.

XII – THE CRUCIFIXION

*Greater love has no man than this,
that a man lay down his life for his friends.*

How many times have we viewed this image? Thousands – probably tens of thousands of time. We walk right past, often not even stopping - pausing to contemplate what it means. The image of Christ crucified is so common to us now that maybe we fail to recognize the great gift it is.

This extraordinary act of love - this gift of love to us. *He did not spare his own Son but gave him up for us all.* Jesus calls those he did not even know friend and died for us all that we might have life. What a gift! What do we do with this gift?

We may not suffer death, but we give up our life when we say "I do" at our wedding or "I will" when we make religious vows. In these promises we are called to die in ways to ourselves for another and follow that command of Christ, *that you love one another as I have loved you.*

For hundreds of years early Christians could not bear to look upon the image of one crucified because of the pain it would cause. Now let us look on it every time as the greatest act of love we have ever witnessed.

— *Patrick Baikauskas, O.P.*

We look upon you Jesus
    in recognition of that great love you have for us.
We ask you to place deep in our hearts
    faith, hope, and love;
    sorrow for our sins,
    and a desire to follow you in everything.
Amen.

XIII – Christ is Taken Down from the Cross and Placed in His Mother's Arms

Who can imagine a more disheartening scene? A mother holds in her arms the lifeless body of her son. The mighty savior and source of hope for a world in need now lies broken, pierced, bloody, limp. How could Mary have endured standing at the foot of the cross, watching her Savior and child die in agony and humiliation?

But here we see in Mary's face not only sadness but also tenderness and strength. While nothing could have prepared her for the shock and intensity of this experience, she had pondered all along the suffering entailed in God becoming man. In loving Jesus so closely, she would share in his suffering as well. We can tell she had been prepared from the start to be the bearer—the carrier—of her Lord. Just look at the way Mary cradles his body as she did the night of his birth.

How incredible this mystery is! Jesus carried all of our sin, our brokenness, our failures, and our mortality upon himself all the way to the cross. When this passionate love stretched humanity to the limit, there remains the faithful love of a mother tenderly supporting the body of her son. Her blue mantle seems to envelop the heavy load she carries, as if heaven supplies the strength her arms could not manage alone. As she carried Jesus, so she carries us, the mystical Body of Christ, with all of our sin, brokenness, failures, and mortality. Because we are one with Christ, Mary is our mother too, upholding us when we are weighed down and too weak to go on, showing us the power of love, which she learned from her son. With sadness tempered by unfailing hope in God's plan, she remains with us, and helps us draw near Jesus in his broken beauty.

— *James Peter Trares, O.P.*

You did not leave us, Lord,
    to face our weakness and sin alone.
Rather, you took it upon yourself
    with unsurpassable love,
    sacrificing your very life for us.
As you gave yourself over to the care
    of your Blessed Mother,
    so you entrust us to her tender care.
Through knowing the woman
    who carried you the closest,
    may we learn to draw close to you,
    especially at our weakest moments.

XIV – Christ is Laid in the Tomb

The horror has ended. The agony has ceased. The mission has been accomplished. The Father's will has been done.

Within the tomb all is silent, lifeless, still. He is cut off from the living. No disciples following Him everywhere, hanging on his every word. No crowds bringing their sick, their maimed, their dead for him to cure, restore, resurrect. No prideful religious leaders confronting him, trying to trick him, to prove him to be a false prophet. The debates are done. The powers of this world appear to have won; jealousy and derision appear to have triumphed.

To his disciples, all seems to be over. They flee in fear lest those who killed the Master should come and kill them too. His promises have come to nothing. Their time spent at his feet has proven to be time wasted. The darkness in their hearts mirrors the darkness of his tomb. They are filled with grieving emptiness. All hope is lost. What will become of us now? they wonder. What are we to do? It is a time of despair, a time for only tears. The fingers of death have constricted their hearts. They have no future. The shock of His cruel death has erased his words of comforting promise from their minds.

But outside the tomb there is light: light by which we are able to see dimly the inert body. Is this light merely the sun? Or might it be the Glory of God encouraging us not to give up like the others, but to wait with hearts full of peace and hope? Is this scene within the tomb meant to be permanent? Or is it just a "time between" – between what has been promised and the fulfillment of the promise? In faith, we who view this scene know the answer, an answer we should never forget should we find ourselves in a tomb hewn of disappointment, disillusionment, betrayal or pain. In such moments let us hear Jesus shouting to us from the tomb: Every ending is a beginning; have hope; I am faithful to my word.

— *Benjamin Russell, O.P.*

O God Who loves us so much
    that you gave your only begotten Son
    to be offered as a sacrifice for our sins
    so that we might spend eternity with You,
please help us ever to remember this truth
    in our darkest moments.
Remind us often that dawn daily follows night
    and that the other side of the tomb is resurrection.
Make us people of living hope.
We ask this through our Savior,
    Jesus Christ the Lord.
Amen.

Concluding Prayer

My Sorrowful & Immaculate Mother,
    lend me your heart
that I may finally love your Son
    as He deserves to be loved.
Grant me a hatred for the sins that afflicted Him
    so brutally,
and inspire me with the courage to imitate
    His heroic sacrifice of love.

Beloved Savior,
    the wounds on your Body are but a reflection
    of the disfigurement sin has wrought in my soul.
I beg you ever to preserve me from the misfortune
    of offending you further.
Teach me what a privilege it is to suffer
    for love of you,
and give me the joy of reigning with you
    in the Glory of your Resurrection,
    with the Father and the Holy Spirit,
You who are One God, for ever and ever.
Amen.

www.ingramcontent.com/pod-product-compliance
Lightning Source LLC
Chambersburg PA
CBHW041808040426
42449CB00001B/9